The Wolfling's Bite

THE NIGHTMARE CLUB

THE WOLFLING'S BITE

ANNIE GRAVES

~~OISÍN MCGANN~~

Little Island

The Wolfling's Bite
First published in 2012 by Little Island Books
This edition first published in 2025
by Little Island Books, New Work Junction,
11 Wynnefield Road, Rathmines,
Dublin, D06 F9C1, Ireland

www.littleisland.ie

ISBN 978-1-915071-81-1

A British Library Cataloguing in Publication record for this book is available from the British Library.

Product safety queries can be addressed to Little Island Books at the above address or info@littleisland.ie

Book design by Someday and Sarah McCoy
Printed in England by CPI

Little Island has received funding to support this book from the Arts Council
of Ireland / An Chomhairle Ealaíon

the arts council an chomhairle ealaíon | funding literature

10 9 8 7 6 5 4 3 2 1

For all my pets — real, toy
and … *possessed*

Annie Graves is twelve years old, and she has no intention of ever growing up. She is, conveniently, an orphan, and lives at an undisclosed address in the Glasnevin area of Dublin with her pet toad, Much Misunderstood, and a small black kitten, Hugh Shalby Nameless.

You needn't think she goes to school — pah! — or has anything as dull as brothers and sisters or hobbies, but let's just say she keeps a large cauldron on the stove.

Publisher's note: We did try to take a picture of Annie, but her face just kept fading away. We have sent our camera for investigation, but suspect the worst.

THANK YOU!

Look, this is my book and I wrote it, even if Jonah was the one who told the story ... Other people do tell the stories, but I'm the one who writes them down, because I'm the author, and that's what I'm good at.

But there's this Oisín McGann person who keeps saying it's really his story, and he is not even Jonah, so I don't know what he's talking about. I hear he has a Wolfling, though, so just to be on the safe side, thanks, Oisín for ... whatever it is you think you have contributed to my story.

And thank you too for buying my book, *dear* reader. You are clearly a person of exquisite taste.

OK, you know how it goes. My house. My friends. Sleepover. everyone tells a story — and it better be scary!

So anyway, this night, the honourable members of the Nightmare Club were sipping the remains of the Rot Chocolate from our cups and chewing on the last few jelly eyeballs.

It was Jonah’s turn to tell a story. He rubbed his stubbly head and blinked tired, hollow eyes. When Jonah started talking, it was like he didn’t *want* to tell this story … but he *had* to …

And this is how it started.

You all know what happened to my little sister, right?

Except you don't.

We stopped trying to tell people what *really* happened to Jessie.

I'm going to tell you now. I'm sick of keeping it a secret. It's like having something eating at your insides.

Remember Jessie got one of those Wolflings for Christmas?

It was a robotic cuddly toy, black and brown, the size of a real wolf puppy.

She fell in love with the thing.

'Twinkle', she called it. Ever heard such a stupid name for a *wolf*?

A Wolfling is one of those learning robots, right?

It learns more sounds and tricks the more you play with it.

It can learn to copy noises you make. Even words you say.

Jessie used to carry Twinkle round in one of Mum's old handbags, with his head poking out. Like the celebrities do with their tiny little dogs. Like he was a fashion accessory or something.

God, I hated that thing.

I started trying to teach him swear words, but he wouldn't respond to my voice. He knew I wasn't his owner.

So I decided to go online and see if there were any cheats, like in a computer game, to see if I could get Twinkle to swear.

That's when I started finding warnings about the Wolflings.

There were all sorts of rumours.

Some said they could move without being switched on.

Some said they could suddenly malfunction and go completely mental, thrashing all over the place.

Some people claimed their Wolflings had *bitten* them.

There were two warnings that came up again and again:

Don't let a Wolfling smell its owner's blood.

and

Don't let it anywhere near meat after sunset.

I read these warnings, but ... well, you know ... it was the *internet*. I didn't take it too seriously.

At least not until the night Jessie screamed.

Long before she was into Wolflings, Jessie got these two rabbits.

She kept them in a hutch in her bedroom.

Roger's right ear was always flopping down. It never stood up straight.

Bugs had the same problem, but with the left ear.

Roger was mostly black and Bugs was mostly white.

They didn't *do* much. Most of the time they just sat there looking dopey. Anyway, it was around midnight one night.

I was still awake, hiding under the covers, playing *Gory Death Killer 4* on my Nintendo. I couldn't get off the level with the mutant chainsaws.

That's when I heard this *shriek* that nearly lifted me out of my bed.

AAAAAAAAGGGHHHHH

I raced to Jessie's bedroom with Mum and Dad close behind me.

Jessie was sitting up in her pink princess bed. In one arm, she was clutching her beloved Twinkle.

She was holding her other hand over her nose. There was blood seeping through her fingers.

'I think Roger bit me!' she squealed. 'I just woke up and something was biting me!'

Mum rushed over with a tissue and pulled Jessie's hand away to look at the wound.

I only got a glimpse of the bite-marks, but they looked pretty nasty.

Roger had somehow bitten her right on the bridge of the nose.

Mum let out a gasp and Dad swore under his breath.

We all looked down at Roger the rabbit, who was out of his cage.

He squatted there, staring up at Jessie with wide eyes. The door of the hutch was unlatched, but Bugs was still inside, shivering in the corner under some straw.

Roger nipped people sometimes, but this was way more serious.

Dad picked up Roger, but he didn't put him back in the hutch. He walked out of the room carrying the rabbit.

Jessie was too upset to notice, but I followed Dad down the stairs.

‘What are you doing, Dad?’ I asked.

‘We can’t keep this animal if he’s going to bite,’ he said.

I didn’t like the way he was calling Roger ‘this animal’.

‘So what are you going to do?’

‘I’m taking him out to the car,’ he replied, without looking at me.

Now, Dad's a really decent guy.

But he can be ... *hard*.

I knew what he was thinking. This rabbit had bitten his princess.

Dad wouldn't stand for that. I'd heard about bad dogs that had been 'sent away to a farm'.

'Dad! No!' I yelled. 'Dad! Please! Please don't!'

He looked at me as he pulled open the back door.

'It has to be done, Jonah. This animal's dangerous. Jessie will understand … eventually. I hope you will too.'

Roger gave me a pleading, despairing look with his big eyes.

Then Dad closed the door firmly behind him and took Roger out to the car.

We never saw Roger the rabbit again.

Jessie was really upset all the next day. She wouldn't come out of her room.

She may be a pain, but she's still my little sister. I went to see if she was all right.

I found her sitting on the floor beside the rabbit hutch. There was a big bandage over her nose. She was cuddling Twinkle and gazing miserably at Bugs.

I sat down beside her and stared down at Bugs.

He stared right back at us. He was really worked up about something.

I thought he could be wondering where Roger was.

Maybe he knew.

Jessie stuck her finger up her nose and picked some of the dried blood from inside her nostril.

(I know, disgusting.)

'Don't *do* that,' I told her. 'You'll make it bleed again.'

She shrugged, but didn't answer.

She kept picking at the dried blood. It's not the first time she'd picked her nose — she was always doing it.

That's when the thought occurred to me.

My mind went back to the warnings I'd read online about the Wolflings.

'Jessie,' I asked, in my kindest voice, 'did you pick your nose last night? Before Roger ... before you got bitten?'

She shrugged again. But when you've known someone their whole life, you can read their shrugs.

'Did you pick at it enough to make it bleed?' I said. 'I mean, *before* you got bitten? Did you give yourself a bleeding nose last night before you went to sleep?'

She didn't even shrug this time.

I stood up and went over to her bed.

I found what I was looking for under her pillow. A tissue with little spots of blood on it.

She *had* picked her nose enough to make it bleed.

DON'T LET A
WOLFLING SMELL
ITS OWNER'S BLOOD,

I'd read on the Internet.

DON'T LET IT
ANYWHERE NEAR MEAT
AFTER SUNSET.

I glanced over at the bandage on my sister's nose, my heart pounding.

Would Jessie's nose count as *meat*?

My gaze fell on Bugs, all alone in his hutch. He was absolutely *terrified*.

And I'd swear, I'd *swear*, that his twitchy little nose was pointing up at the cuddly toy wolf cub cradled in my sister's arms.

He was *pointing* at Twinkle the Wolfling.

After dinner that evening, I went online again, pretending I was working on a school project. Instead, I looked up Wolflings.

There were the warnings again. Some said that these robotic toys could be driven into a frenzy by the smell of blood in darkness. Some said that Wolflings were made out of the skins of werewolves.

'Go to bed, honey,' Mum said. 'You look really tired. You need to get some sleep.'

As if I could sleep, knowing what I knew!

I looked in on Jessie before I went to bed.

'Hey, Jess, I was just . . . you know . . . just thinking. Maybe you shouldn't sleep with Twinkle like that, huh? Maybe we should put him in the rabbit hutch with Bugs.'

I thought I heard Bugs give a whimper, but I couldn't be sure.

Jessie scowled at me, grasping the Wolfling to her cheek. 'But he's *guarding* me, Jonah! He's keeping me safe!'

'Right,' I said. 'Right, OK.'

I didn't know what to do.

If I told her what I'd read, she'd only get nightmares. Mum would kill me for scaring my little sister.

I lay in bed, clutching the duvet up close to my face. It took me hours to fall asleep.

Jessie was sobbing loudly when I woke up the next morning. She sounded heartbroken.

I could hear Mum trying to comfort her.

I crept into her room, afraid of what I'd find.

She and Mum were sitting on the bed. They hardly noticed me.

It took me a minute to figure out what was wrong.

Bugs was gone.

The door of the hutch was latched shut, but there was a hole in the wire mesh of the cage.

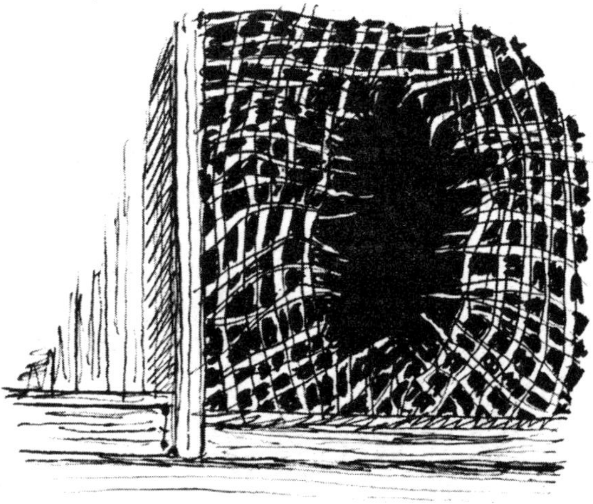

'He must have run away,' Mum said. 'I don't know how he got out of the house. Oh, I'm so sorry, honey.'

The hole in the cage was big enough for a rabbit to get out.

Or something else to get in.

I leaned in closer, peering through the mesh.

There were tufts of fur on the floor of the cage, and a few drops of blood.

I turned my head and stared at the cuddly wolf cub that Jessie was squeezing tight to her.

I'd swear it stared right back at me.

Bugs hadn't run away. I was sure of that.

Enough was enough – it was time to get rid of Twinkle.

By nightfall, I knew what I needed to do.

I was going to wait until Jessie was asleep, then I was going to take the Wolfling from her arms.

I'd take him out to the garden shed.

Jessie always slept with just a night light, with the door closed.

I slipped quietly into her room.

I crept over to her bed. She was fast asleep, with Twinkle clutched in her arms.

But as I leaned over her, she stuck her finger up her nose and started poking around in that nostril full of scabbed blood.

There was a quiet growl.

Twinkle turned his head to look up at me. He knew what I was there to do.

He moved so suddenly, I barely saw it.

As fast as a cat striking, he was on me.

He opened jaws that were *way* too big for his head.

Jaws full of metal teeth.

I squealed and just managed to stop him biting my face, but he twisted and clamped his teeth into my arm instead.

I shrieked again.

Jessie was awake now, staring in shock and terror.

SHR

She has guts, my little sister. She grabbed the Wolfling and pulled him off me, throwing him across the room.

He bounced off the wall and landed on his feet.

He let out a savage snarl.

He went for Jessie then, leaping straight at her face.

She turned just as he hit her, and this time it was *me* who had to pull him off *her*.

She screamed when I did, grabbing at the side of her head.

I slammed the thing onto the floor as hard as I could.

SLAM

He went to squirm away, but I lifted up the rabbit hutch and brought it crashing down on the Wolfling.

He was stunned, but that wasn't enough.

I don't know
how many times
I smashed at him
with that hutch.

I kept doing it until
Dad grabbed it
from me and
hugged me to him.

Jessie was still screaming.

There was blood all over her shoulder …

We were all looking at Jonah, but nobody was saying anything.

After a moment, Jonah went on …

The police wouldn't believe our story when we told them.

And the company that makes the Wolflings said we couldn't prove that Twinkle had really attacked us.

People laughed at us.

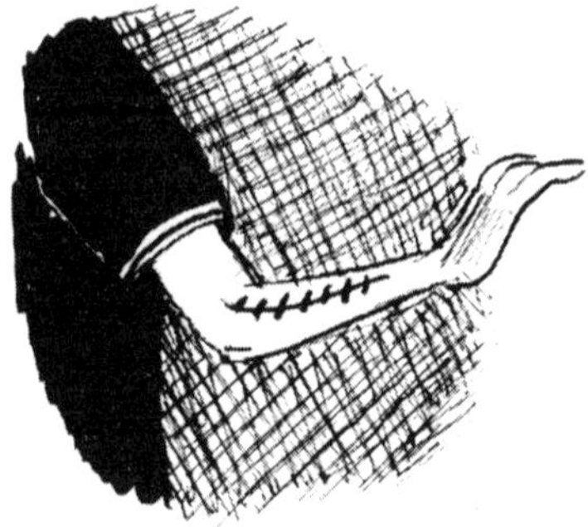

So the story we tell now is that Jessie and I were attacked by a stray dog.

Jonah pulled up his sleeve so we could see the scar on his arm from a bite-mark.

‘So now you know how I really got this scar,’ he said. ‘And you know how my sister ended up with *only one ear*.’

The Wolfling *bit off the other one*.’

Jonah went quiet then.

He didn't talk again for a long time.

Nobody did.

But the thing is ... there's more of those things out there – *hundreds of thousands* of them.

And if Jonah's story is true, all it takes is the smell of their owner's blood in the darkness ... and ...

THE END